Mike Phillips

To Craig Lye, a Prince among interns

Our books are tested
for children and young people by
children and young people.

Thanks to everyone who consulted on
a manuscript for their time and effort in
helping us to make our books better
for our readers.

First published in 2012 in Great Britain by
Barrington Stoke Ltd
18 Walker Street, Edinburgh, EH3 7LP

www.barringtonstoke.co.uk

ISBN: 978-1-78112-231-0

Printed in the UK by Bell & Bain

Contents

Chapter 1

Amazing Athletes

Jessica Ennis
The Face of the Games

Jessica Ennis became the 'Face of the Games' in the run-up to the London 2012 Olympics. She was in TV adverts and on posters. When she walked into the Olympic Stadium for her first event, the whole country thought, 'Can she win gold?'

Jessica wasn't able to take part in the 2008 Olympic Games in Beijing because she had hurt her foot. She was really upset about missing the Games, but she came back in 2009 and won the World Championships. In 2010 she won the World Indoor Championships with a record score! At the 2011 World Championships she finished in 2nd place, and she lost her World Champion title. But she did get an MBE from the Queen that same year!

The big question was how would she do in the London Olympics?

Jessica's Event

The Women's Heptathlon was first held at the Olympics in 1984. It is made up of seven events, and it takes two days to complete.

On Day 1, the athletes:
1.   run the 100m hurdles
2.   see how high they can jump in the High Jump
3.   throw the shot as far as they can in the shot put
4.   run the 200m as fast as they can

On Day 2, the athletes:

5. see how far they can jump in the Long Jump
6. throw the javelin as far as they can
7. run 800m as fast as they can

Athletes are given points based on how well they perform in each event

Jessica in London

It's 3/8/2012. The first Women's Heptathlon event is about to start – the 100m hurdles. Jessica lines up with the others on the start line.

BANG!

"Go, Jess, go!" the crowd cheers.

Jessica wins! She wins in 12.54 seconds, a new Personal Best! She's in the lead, with 1,195 points!

Next it's the High Jump. Jessica finishes 5th, and scores 1,054 points. But she's still in the lead overall.

Shot Put is next, and Jessica only manages to throw 14.28m, a score of 813 points. She drops down to 2nd overall!

The 200m is the last event of the day. "Come on Jess!" the crowd shouts. Can she end today in 1st place?

Yes, she can! Jessica wins the 200m in a time of 22.83 seconds. She scores 1,096 points and takes back the lead.

The next day, Jessica comes 2nd in the long jump, with a distance of 6.48m. 1,001 points!

In the javelin, she makes another Personal Best at 47.49m. She is only in 10th place, but her score of 812 points means she's still 1st overall.

Now there's only the 800m race left. The crowd goes wild, chanting Jessica's name and whistling. The race starts with a BANG and they're off! In the last 100m she sprints far in front of the other runners, and wins in 2 minutes 8 seconds! She is amazing!

Jessica is the overall winner, scoring 6,955 points. Gold medal for Jessica Ennis!

Mo Farah
Magic Mo-ment

Mo Farah was the only hope Britain had to win a long distance medal in the 2012 Olympics. He was going to run the 10,000m and the 5,000m races. If he won, it would be the first time Britain had ever won gold in men's long distance running. Could he do it?

At the Beijing Olympics, Mo didn't make it into the final of the 5,000m. He promised that he would do whatever it took to become the best in the world. He went to Africa over the winter to train in the mountains, where his body could get used to working with less oxygen. This made him a better runner and in 2010, he won his first major title – the 10,000m in the European Athletics Championships. In 2011, he moved to America to train with a new coach, and won the silver medal in the 10,000m at the World Championships.

Mo's Events

The first time the 10,000m was in the Olympics was in 1912. It is the longest track event. The runner must finish 25 laps of the track – equal to just over six miles! In the 5,000m the runner must finish 12.5 laps of the track.

Mo in London

It's 4/8/2012. The final of the 10,000m is here at last. Mo lines up with the other runners. Jessica Ennis and Greg Rutherford have already won gold medals today. Can Mo do the same?

"Set," says the starter.

BANG!

The race is on! The runners set out at a fast pace, but Mo knows it won't be as fast all the way. Mo settles in. There's still a long way to go! He runs alongside the current world champion, about the middle of the pack. After 5,000m, the pace gets faster, and Mo begins to move toward the front of the group. With 800m to go, Mo goes for it, and takes the lead! He runs ahead of the pack around the track for two whole laps. He crosses the line first, with a time of 27 minutes and 30 seconds! It's a gold medal for Mo Farah!

Exactly one week later, Mo lines up for the 5,000m race. The gun goes off, and Mo lets the other runners go off in front of him. He stays at the back for three laps, as the runners jog round the track at a slow pace. On the 4th lap, Mo moves to the front of the pack, then moves back to the middle. For the next few laps, he goes between the front and the middle. With three laps to go, the speed gets a lot faster and Mo moves into second place. At the start of the second-last lap, he moves into first place, ready for the big sprint at the end. On the final lap, Mo builds up his speed. With 200m to go, he is running as hard as he can. Nobody can touch him! Mo wins by 5m in a time of 13:44.66.

TWO long distance golds for Mo Farrah!

Chapter 2

Wheels of Fortune

Laura Trott
Princess of the Velodrome

Laura Trott was only 20 years old at the start of the 2012 Olympics. Team GB's cycling team had always done well in the Olympic Games. Could Laura live up to that?

Laura's life was difficult from birth. She was born a month early with a collapsed lung and later she had asthma. Doctors advised her to take up sport and Laura chose cycling. At age 18 she won the European Track Championships in the Team Pursuit event. At

19 she won the gold medal at the European Track Championships in the Team Pursuit and the Omnium. In 2012 she won gold at the World Championships for the same two events.

Laura's Events

The Omnium is a series of six events:

1. a 250m flying start time trial, where riders get their bikes up to speed for a few laps before they start the timed lap
2. a 5km race, where the winner is the first person over the line
3. a knock-out race, where the last rider is knocked out at the end of some laps
4. an individual pursuit, where two riders chase one another round from opposite sides of the track
5. a 10km points race, where cyclists gain points for their position at various parts of the race
6. a 500m time-trial, where the rider with the fastest time wins

The first place rider in each of these events gets one point, the second two points and so on. The winner of the Omnium is the rider with the fewest points.

The Team Pursuit race is simpler. For women, the distance is 3km, or 12 laps of the velodrome. Two teams of three riders start on opposite sides of the track. The winner is the team that either sets the fastest time, or passes the other team.

Laura in London

4/8/12. In the Team Pursuit final, Laura races with Dani King and Joanna Rowsell. The other team is from the USA. The cyclists sit on opposite sides of the velodrome, waiting to start. They're off! The two teams thunder around the circuit, and Team GB pulls ahead after the first lap. The Americans are already 0.669 seconds behind! After the first km, the Americans are 1.104 seconds behind – Team

GB is gaining on them! With one lap to go, Team GB are less than 80m behind – can they catch the American riders? They don't catch them, but they do win the race AND they set a new world record of 3:14.051 minutes! The Americans were more than five seconds behind. What a race.

Three days later, and Laura has had a great start in the Omnium. In the 250m flying start time trial, she came 1st with a time of 14.057 seconds. The rider in 2nd place was just 0.001 seconds slower! In the points race, she scored 14 points. This ranked her 10th, so her overall score was now at 11 points. The third event was the knock-out race, which Laura won! In the individual pursuit Laura came 2nd with a time of 3:30.547. Her Omnium points total is now 14 and she is 2nd overall! In the points race she comes 3rd, missing out on a better place when she was forced to swing wide on the final corner. 17 points! In the time trial, Laura wins in a time of 35.110, just 0.004 seconds ahead of the rider in 2nd place. She's done it! Laura has won gold by one point in the Omnium!

Sir Chris Hoy
The Greatest British Olympian

Sir Chris Hoy is Britain's most famous cyclist. At the London 2012 Opening Ceremony he carried the flag for Great Britain. The nation expected Chris to win lots of medals, like he did in Beijing. Could he do it?

Chris finished the 2008 Beijing Olympics with three gold medals. He was the first British athlete for 100 years to do this. He won the Keirin, the team sprint, and the individual sprint. Chris continued his good form into the 2008-9 season, winning gold in the team sprint in the World Cup. But in the Keirin at the World Cup, he crashed and was hurt. He couldn't race for three months.

In 2009, Chris Hoy was made a knight and became Sir Chris Hoy. In the 2010 world cup, Chris won the gold medal in the Keirin event. At the 2012 World Cup he won the Keirin and the individual sprint. The nation's hopes were high for the Olympics!

Chris's Events

The Men's Team sprint is three laps long. There are two teams on opposite sides of the velodrome, with three riders in each team. At the end of every lap, one rider in each team peels away from his teammates and leaves them to finish the race. On the last lap, one rider is left in each team. The winner is the team with the fastest time.

Keirin means 'racing wheels' in Japanese and began in Japan as a betting sport. The Keirin first appeared in the Olympics in 2000, at Sydney, Australia. The race is 2km long. Riders follow a motor-powered bike called a 'derny' round the track. The derny sets the speed of the race, starting at 25km per hour and rising to 50km per hour. About 600m from the end, the derny draws off the track, and the riders sprint to the finish line.

Chris in London

2/8/12. The Team Sprint final is Britain against France. The British team is Philip Hindes, Jason Kenney and Chris Hoy. The race starts and Britain and France both power away from the line. After one 250m lap, Britain scores a time of 17.274 seconds, with France only 0.005 seconds behind. One rider from Britain and France leave the race. At the end of the second lap, Britain has a time of 29.635 seconds, and France is 0.275 seconds behind.

Two more riders peel off. Can Chris win the race? He storms over the line in a time of 42.6 seconds – a new world record! France finished 0.413 seconds later. Gold for GB!

7/8/12. The Keirin begins slowly as the derny pulls away. After 1km, Chris is in 4th place. Is he too far behind to make it? The derny pulls off the track after three laps and the race is on! The riders storm out, and Chris overtakes them all! But the German rider begins to overtake Chris on the last lap. Chris holds the inside line and pedals as hard as he can. He's 1st! Gold medal for Sir Chris Hoy!

Chapter 3

Terrific Tennis

Andy Murray
Great Scot!

Andy Murray planned a busy Olympic Games. He entered three events: the men's doubles with his younger brother Jamie; the mixed doubles with Laura Robson; and the men's singles. He was the British Number 1 tennis player but he had never won a Grand Slam in his career. Could he do the unthinkable? Could he win gold?

Andy has been the British Number 1 since Tim Henman retired from tennis in 2007. He is playing at a time when there are lots of great tennis players, like Rafael Nadal, Novak Djokovic and Roger Federer. Just three weeks before the Olympics, Andy got into the final at Wimbledon for the first time. Federer beat him in four sets, and Andy took home the runner-up plate. Could he go one better at the Olympics?

Andy's Event

Tennis has been played at every Olympic Games since 1988. At London 2012, the tennis was held at Wimbledon.

In Men's Olympic tennis, matches in the early rounds have three sets. The men's singles final has five sets. The first player to win three sets wins.

Andy in London

5/8/12. Andy Murray and Roger Federer walk out onto Wimbledon's Centre Court to loud cheers from the crowd. They warm up and then they begin play. In the 6th game, Murray breaks Federer's serve – he wins the game even though Federer is serving. It's 4-2 to Murray! Murray breaks Federer's serve again in the 8th game. Murray wins the first set 6-2.

The second set is incredible to watch. Murray wins almost every game, breaking Federer's serve twice, and wins the set 6-1. Murray's two sets up! Only one more needed to win!

The final set is tense. The audience is on edge. If Murray wins this set, he wins the gold medal! Federer seems to be back on form, winning his service games. But then, in the 5th game, Murray breaks Federer! 3-2 to Murray. Federer holds out until the 10th game, when Murray breaks him again and wins the set, 6-4. Game, set, match and championship to Murray! He's done it, he's finally won a big event! 6-2, 6-1, 6-4. Go Andy Murray!

Chapter 4

Britannia Rules the Waves

Katherine Grainger
A Silver Lining ...

In the last three Olympics, Katherine Grainger won a silver medal each time. Katherine didn't want another silver in 2012. She was hungry for gold! As she got into the boat at Eton Dorney lake, she was determined to achieve her dream.

Katherine took part in the last three Olympic Games, in Sydney, Athens and Beijing. She was happy with her first two silver medals.

She was not so happy with her third. Could she ever win gold?

In 2010, Katherine met her new rowing partner, Anna Watkins. They were great friends from the off. Their training went well, and soon you could see that there was something special about them. They began to win race after race after race. They even won the World Championships in 2010 and 2011.

By the time of London 2012, Katherine and Anna had won over 20 races. How could they lose?

Katherine's Event

The Women's Double Sculls is a rowing event for two women. 'Sculls' means that each person in the boat rows with two oars. (If you row with one oar, it is called 'Sweeping'.)

Every race is 2,000m long. The first boat to cross the finish line wins.

Katherine in London

The race starts at Eton Dorney lake, and Britain begins to pull ahead. After five minutes and 1,500m of rowing, Grainger and Watkins are first. There is a whole boat length between them and the nearest boat, Australia. From then on, there is no doubt – Britain is going to take the gold! They finish in a time of 6:55 minutes. A gold medal at last for Katherine Grainger!

Ben Ainslie
Lord of the Sea

Ben Ainslie is one of Britain's sailors.
Before the 2012 Olympics, he had won six world
titles in Finn Class sailing, and three Olympic
Gold medals. Could he make it four?

Ben Ainslie CBE has taken part in Olympic
Games since the 1996 Games in the USA, where
he won a silver medal. In every Olympic Games
since then, (2000, 2004, 2008) he has won the
gold medal. He was World Champion between
2002 and 2005, and then again in 2008 and
2012. Could Ben win another gold medal in the
Olympics, and make it four golds?

Ben's Event

The Finn Class race was first held at the
Olympic Games in 1952. Only one sailor sails
a Finn Class Boat. In an Olympic Finn Class
competition, each boat takes part in 10 races.

The winner of each race gets one point, second place two points and so on. The worst race score for each boat does not count. The ten boats with the lowest scores go on to the medal race. In this race, the points are doubled, so the winner will score two points, 2nd place four points and so on. The sailor with the lowest overall score wins.

The races take place in the open waters of the sea. Sailors must sail around a marked course.

Ben in London

5/8/12. When he goes into the medal race, Ben is in 2nd place. In his first two races, he came 2nd, and so he scored two points in each. In his 3rd race he scored six points. In his 4th race, he scored 12 points – he needed to discount that one! In his 5th and 6th races he scored four and three points. He won his 7th race, so that was a total of 30 points, and put him in 2nd place overall! In his 8th and 9th race he scored three and six points. He won his 10th race. 40 points in total. After his score of 12 points is discounted, he went into the medal race with a score of 28 points. He'll need to work hard to win the medal race!

Ben doesn't have a good race in the medal race. He finishes in 9th place. Because the scores are doubled in the medal race, this gives him eighteen points. But the sailor in first place going into the medal race finished in 10th, with 20 points. This means that Ben is tied with the leader on 46 points! Because

Ben did better in the medal race, he steals the Gold medal! Ben Ainslie is a four-time Olympic Champion!

Chapter 5

The Best of the Rest

Nicola Adams
The Fighter

Nicola Adams is a female boxer. 2012 was the first year women's boxing has been in the Olympics, and so the first ever gold medal was up for grabs! Nicola had been a rising star of women's boxing for years – could she win a gold medal?

Nicola Adams began boxing at the age of 12, but found it hard to find other girl boxers to fight her. In 2007, she won silver in the European Championships. She won silver in the World Championships in 2008 and 2010. In 2011, she managed to win a gold medal in the European Championships. How would she do at the Olympics?

Nicola's Event

Boxing is held in classes according to weight. Nicola is a 'flyweight' boxer, because she weighs under 51kg. Women's boxing matches have four rounds of two minutes each.

To score a point, boxers must land a punch to the face or upper body of their opponent. The boxer with the most points wins!

Nicola in London

9/8/12. It's the final of the women's boxing. Nicola faces Ren Cancan of China, the three-times world number one. Round 1 starts slowly, as each boxer sizes the other up. They both begin to land some serious punches, but Nicola has a higher score at the end of the round – 4-2. The bell rings and Round 2 starts. Nicola is dominant, landing blow after blow on Ren. After a minute of boxing, Nicola does an amazing move. She leans back, letting Ren come in to attack. Then Nicola moves forwards and lands a hefty punch on Ren's arm, followed by a full-on punch to the face. Ren loses her balance and falls to the canvas. A knock-down! The crowd goes wild – surely she can't lose!

After Round 2 the score is 9-5. Round 3 passes in a flurry of punches. Ren can't respond to Nicola. Now the score is 14-5. In the last round, Nicola becomes more careful. She knows she has done enough to win, so long as she doesn't let Ren score. She focuses on defence as she waits for the seconds to tick down. There goes the bell! The MC announces in a loud voice that the winner of the first Olympic women's boxing gold medal is ... Nicola Adams, with a score of 16-7! Gold medal for Nicola Adams!

Tom Daley
Making a Splash...

Tom Daley is one of the most famous faces of the games. In the run-up to London 2012, he was in lots of adverts and on lots of talk shows. But poor Tom had to study for his A-Level exams, too! As he climbed to the 10m platform for the singles final, the nation watched.

Tom took part in the 2008 Olympics in Beijing, where he came 7th in the 10m platform competition. In 2009, he won the FINA world championships in Rome. In 2010 he and his team-mate Max Brick won the gold medal for the 10m synchronised dive in the Commonwealth Games. In November 2010, Tom won the BBC Young Sports Personality of the Year Award for the third time. Going into the Olympic Games, he had the hopes of the nation resting on his shoulders.

Tom's Event

Diving competitions are held at a number of different heights above the water. Tom Daley competes in the 10m platform dive. Men must complete six dives. Each dive they perform is given a difficulty rating depending on the elements in the dive. Three judges award the dive a score out of ten. This score is then multiplied by the difficulty factor to give an overall score for the dive.

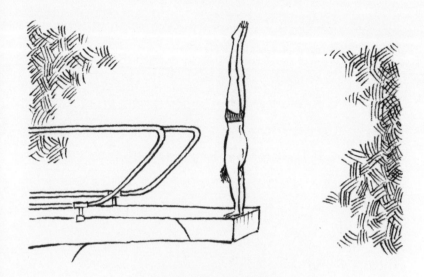

Tom in London

11/8/12. Tom has made it to the finals of the 10m platform diving competition. He qualified in 15th place in the early rounds. In the semi-finals, he moved up to 4th place.

Tom's first dive in the final is very dramatic. When he dives, people in the crowd take pictures with flash. The flashes put Tom off, and ruin the dive. He asks the referee for a redive, and is allowed to go again! On his second attempt he scores 91.80!

Tom's 3rd dive is more tricky. He has to do a handstand on the platform, and then three back somersaults (difficulty 3.5). He scores 92.75. In the 4th dive, things change a lot. First, Tom performs his best dive – 4.5 somersaults (difficulty 3.7) – and scores 98.05. This moves him up into 3rd position overall, with a score of 369.00. Then the two Chinese divers, who dive after Tom, both make mistakes. This lowers their score by a lot. Tom might win it!

On Tom's 5th dive, 3.5 back somersaults (difficulty 3.6), Tom scores 97.20, which moves him up into 1st place. But his final dive doesn't have a high enough difficulty rating to win – he is only able to score 90.75. This score isn't enough to beat the American diver, Bodia, or the Chinese diver Qiu. Tom finishes in 3rd place with a score of 556.95. Bodia won with a score of 568.65, and Qiu scored 566.85. A bronze medal for Tom Daley!

Beth Tweddle
A Medal for Tweddle?

Beth Tweddle is one of the most successful British gymnasts there has ever been. She was one of the faces of the London 2012 games. But she had never won an Olympic Medal before.

Beth is the most decorated British gymnast ever. She has been European Champion four times (2006, 2009, 2010, 2011), and World

Champion three times (2006, 2009, 2010). In the Olympics in Athens she came 10th, in Beijing, she came 4th. Could Tweddle get a medal before she retired?

Beth's Event

Beth competed on the uneven bars in London. The uneven bars are two bars set at different heights above the ground – the low bar is 1.7m high and the high bar is 2.5m high. The bars are 1.8m apart. Judges then award the gymnast a mark out of ten for how well they perform their routine on the bars. Each routine is also awarded a difficulty rating. The mark out of ten is added to the difficulty rating to provide the final score.

Beth in London

6/8/12. It's the final of the women's uneven bars. Beth vaults onto the top bar and begins her routine. She spins round with grace, moving between the top and bottom bars. Each routine must contain twists, changes of grip, as well as flying elements. Beth's has lots of all of these.

Beth swings around the high bar ready to jump down. But she lands awkwardly and has to take a large step back to balance herself. At least she doesn't fall! The judges score her routine at a difficulty of 7.000 and an execution score of 8.916. A total of 15.916 puts her 2nd behind He Kexin of China.

Aliya Mustafina of Russia goes next, and scores a huge 16.133, jumping to the top of the leader board ahead of He and Beth. Beth finishes in third place – a bronze for Beth! An Olympic medal at last for Beth Tweddle!

Chapter 6

The Paralympics
Meet the Superhumans!

Ellie Simmonds
Golden girl!

The opening ceremony for the London 2012 Paralympic Games took place on Wednesday 29 August. One of the athletes who walked out into the stadium was Ellie Simmonds. She was only 18 years old. Ellie suffers from a genetic disorder that causes dwarfism. She is only 1.23m tall. Ellie had been in lots of adverts on TV for the Paralympics, and everyone wanted her to do well. Could she swim her way to a gold medal?

Ellie took part in the Beijing Olympics in 2008 when she was just 13 years old. She was the youngest British athlete at the Paralympics. She took part in several events, like the 50m butterfly and the 200m IM, and she won gold medals in the 100m freestyle and the 400m freestyle. When she came to the London Games, she wanted to defend her titles. Could she do it?

Ellie's Events

All athletes that take part in the Paralympics are put into different classes, to make sure that all the athletes compete against people who are disabled in a similar way to themselves. This means that the Paralympics are fair for everyone. Ellie competes in the S6 and SM6 class of swimming. 'S' means either front-crawl, backstroke or butterfly. 'SM' stands for the medley. The 6 is a number given to athletes between one and ten

to say how serious their disability is. The lower
the number, the more serious the disability.

Ellie in London

1/9/12. Ellie's first event is the 400m
freestyle. As she walks out to the pool, the roar
from the crowd is deafening! As she stands on
the blocks, the noise dies down.

"Take your marks" says the commentator.

'Beep' goes the starting box – and off they
go!

Ellie starts well and stays with the pack for the first 100m. She goes into 2nd place and stays as close as she can to the swimmer in 1st. Together, they begin to pull away from the rest. With 100m to go, Ellie makes a break and speeds up to lead the pack. The crowd is on its feet, cheering her on. With 25m to go, she manages to take 1st place, and keeps pulling away. Come on Ellie! Yes! Ellie has won gold and set a new World Record of 5 minutes and 19.17 seconds. Well done, Ellie!

Ellie's next event is the 200m IM. The race begins, and Ellie is quite far back on the butterfly leg as the taller swimmers pull away with their longer arms. On the backstroke length, Ellie begins to come back through the pack. By the breaststroke length, she is in 2nd place! You can do it Ellie! As soon as she starts the front crawl length, Ellie speeds past the swimmer in 1st place and pulls away. She's won! And she's set a new World Record of

3 minutes 05.39. A second gold medal for Ellie Simmonds!

Ellie also competed in the 50m freestyle, where she won a bronze medal. In the 100m freestyle, she won a silver medal with a time of 1:14.82, a new British record!

David Weir
The Weir Wolf

David Weir, also called 'The Weir Wolf', has been taking part in Paralympic Games since the 1996 Games in Atlanta. He was born with a problem with his spine, which means he can't use his legs. He now races in a wheelchair. At the 2012 Paralympic Games, Weir was 33 years old, but still winning races. Everyone expected him to win several Olympic Gold medals – could he do it?

At the Atlanta Games in 1996, David competed in the 100m and finished 7th. In the London Marathon in 2000, he finished 4th. He has taken part in every London marathon since, and has now won six times! At the Athens Games in 2004, he won a silver for the 100m, and a bronze for the 200m. In Beijing in 2008, he competed in the longer track events – the 400m, 800m, 1,500m, and 5,000m. He won gold in the 800m and 1,500m, silver in the 400m and bronze in the 5,000m. By 2011, he was the World Champion in the 800m, 1,500m, and the 5,000m. Going into the London Paralympic Games, he wanted to show everyone he still had it.

David's Events

Like Ellie, David was placed in a 'class' due to his disability. His class was T54 class. T means Track. Numbers are given to make sure racers with similar disabilities race each other. For wheelchair racing, the numbers are between 51 and 54. The number 54 means that the athlete can move his legs a little bit by himself, and has no problems with his arms. The numbers 51-53 are for athletes who are disabled in both their legs and their arms. The lower the number is, the more serious the disability.

David in London

2/9/12 David's first event is the 5,000m – 12.5 laps of a 400m track. David lines up with the other athletes, waiting for the gun to go off.

'Bang!'

They're off!

There is an early sprint from one of the other racers. David chases after him and moves into 3rd place right away. He stays in 3rd for a couple of laps, then drops back to the middle of the pack to rest his arms for a short while. Everyone in the pack plays their part in keeping the pace high. With five laps to go, David moves into 4th, and waits for his moment to strike. With 500m to go, David follows a break and moves up into 2nd. Come on David!

It comes down to a last lap sprint! With 200m to go, David pulls level with the racer in first place. The crowd is on its feet, roaring him on. With 100m to go, David pulls away by a length and storms across the line with a clear lead. He's won his first gold medal of the 2012 Paralympic Games, in a time of 11 minutes 07.65 seconds!

The 1,500m is David's next race. This event is 3.75 laps of a 400m track, and is a very fast race for wheelchair racers. The race starts, and David sits close to the front, sometimes 2nd and sometimes 3rd. He can't drop too far back, or he won't have a chance to make it to the front! With 400m to go, David moves into first place. With 250m to go, he makes an early break for the line, and sprints away from the rest of the field. No one can catch him, and he wins in a time of 3 minutes, 12.08 seconds. A second gold medal for David Weir!

David's last track event is the 800m. This race is only two laps long, and very fast. David starts in lane 7. The gun goes off, and he pulls right into 2nd behind a Chinese racer. The pack becomes bunched at the front, and with 200m to go they are racing in a line! David decides to go wide with 200m to go, pushing with all his might to get into first. Can he do it? Come on, David!! There's 50m to go! He's pulling into first place! Yes! The Weir Wolf crosses the line first for his third gold medal, with a time of 1minute and 37.63 seconds. Well done, David!

David's final event is the marathon. After racing for almost an hour and a half, the athletes turn onto the Mall, in front of Buckingham Palace. David is in the lead. He puts on a burst of speed, but it's clear that no one can catch him. He crosses the line in first place, with a time of 1 hour, 30 minutes and 20 seconds. Four gold medals for David Weir at the London 2012 Olympic Games!

Chapter 7

International Superstars

Michael Phelps
Lord of the Gold Rush

London 2012 was going to be Michael Phelps' last Olympic Games. At the Games in Beijing, he had won eight gold medals. This was more than anyone had ever won in a single Olympic Games. As he walked out to the pool in London, everyone wondered, 'what is he going to do this time?'

Michael's first Olympic Games was at Athens in 2004, where he won six gold medals and two bronzes. He was only 19! At his second

Games, in Beijing, he won eight gold medals. He also broke seven world records and one Olympic record. At the London 2012 Olympics, he entered seven events. The four individual events were the 100m butterfly, the 200m individual medley, the 400m individual medley and the 200m butterfly. The three relay events were the 4 x 200m freestyle relay, the 4 x 100m medley relay and the 4 x 100m freestyle relay. How many golds would he get this time?

Michael's Events

Swimming has been a part of the Olympic Games since the first Games in 1896. In those Olympics, the races were held in the Mediterranean Sea! In 1904, the backstroke races were added. Butterfly races were added in 1956. Women's swimming was introduced in 1912. There are four strokes that are used in the Olympic Games – front crawl, backstroke, butterfly and breaststroke. All four strokes can be combined into an Individual Medley race. In relays, teams of four race over 200m, 400m, or 800m distances. Olympic races are all held in a 50m pool.

Michael in London

Michael's first event was the 400m Individual Medley. He was 2nd after the butterfly. But on the backstroke and breaststroke legs, he fell further and further behind. His teammate Ryan Lochte was pulling away, and Phelps couldn't keep up with him. By the start of the front crawl leg, Phelps was 4th, and he stayed in that position until the end. No one could believe it. Was this a sign of things to come?

The next day, Phelps swam as part of the 4 x 100m front crawl relay team. He swam the second leg. He gave the team a lead over the other swimmers, which the USA kept until the final leg. Then the last French swimmer stormed down the pool and overtook Ryan

Lochte, the last American. The French won by 0.45 seconds. Silver to the USA.

In Michael's 200m butterfly race, he swam as hard as he could, but Chad le Clos from South Africa beat him by just 0.05 seconds. Silver for Phelps! In the 4 x 200m front crawl relay he won his first gold of 2012. With that gold medal he became the record holder for the most Olympic medals won.

Over the next few days, Michael won a gold medal in the 200m Individual Medley with a time of 1 minute 54.27 seconds. He won a gold medal in the 100m butterfly with a time of 51.21 seconds. His final event was the 4 x 100m medley relay. He swam the third leg – the butterfly. As he entered the pool, he was second, just behind Japan. But he stormed through the water and overtook the Japanese swimmer 10m from the end of the pool. The front crawl swimmer held the lead to win a gold medal for the USA, and a gold medal for the last race of Michael's career!

Michael Phelps left London with 22 Olympic medals – 18 gold, 2 silver and 2 bronze. He was presented with a special trophy to commemorate his amazing achievement.

Usain Bolt
The Fastest Man on Earth

Usain Bolt changed the face of short distance sprinting. His electric personality and cool attitude on the track brought the race to life for the fans. The 100m was the most popular event at London 2012 – everyone wanted a ticket to see the fastest man alive. But Usain had doubted himself since the Beijing Olympics. Would Usain pull it off again, or would he be beaten?

Usain broke onto the world athletics stage at the Beijing Olympics. He recorded a new world record time for the 100m of 9.69 seconds – when he was slowing down! He also recorded a new world record in the 200m of 19.30 seconds. But after Beijing, things didn't go as well as he would have liked. In 2011 he was disqualified from the 100m World Championships for a false start. This was a major blow. It also gave a boost to Yohan Blake, also from Jamaica. Everyone knew that Yohan was fast, but was he faster than Bolt? Would London 2012 see Bolt beaten on the biggest stage? Or would he do something that had never been done before, and defend his 100m and 200m titles from Beijing?

Bolt's Events

The 100m sprint was first run in an Olympic Games in 1896. The winner of the 100m sprint is considered to be the fastest man on the planet. The 200m was first held at the Olympics in 1900. Sprinters in these races can average speeds of 20mph over the race. A top speed might be closer to 25mph. Usain Bolt's top speed is about 27mph.

In the 4x100m sprint, a team of four runners sprints 100m each. The first runner starts with a baton, which he then passes to the second runner and so on. The baton must always be in the hand of the racing runner.

Bolt in London

5/8/12. The sprinters line up for the 100m. The crowd is completely silent, waiting for the start. The starter's pistol fires, and the race begins! Usain Bolt is not the quickest out of the blocks. At 50m, all the sprinters are running beside each other. Then, at the 80m mark, Usain begins to pull away from the others. He crosses the line about five metres ahead of Yohan Blake, in a time of 9.63 seconds. It's a new Olympic Record! He's done it! Gold medal

for Usain Bolt, and Yohan Blake takes the silver. The crowd goes wild!

Four days later, Usain is back in the stadium for the 200m. If he wins this race, he will be the first man to win both the 100m and 200m at two Olympic Games, one after another. Can he do it? The race starts and Usain powers around the track. It's clear that no one can catch him and he storms away. He crosses the line in a time of 19.32 – another gold medal! Usain Bolt is the double double Olympic Champion. He's an Olympic legend!

One week after the 100m, Usain takes part in the 4 x 100m relay. The Jamaicans are quick and slick, and they win in a new World Record time of 36.84 seconds! Three gold medals for Usain Bolt! He is the fastest man alive. What will he do next?

The 2012 London Games were an incredible success. Britain won 29 gold medals, 17 silver medal and 19 bronze medals – 65 medals in total! This meant that Britain came 3rd overall in the medal tables, behind the USA and China. Every British athlete who won a medal said how amazing it had been to win in front of a home crowd. At the Closing Ceremony, Boris Johnson, the Mayor of London, handed the Olympic flag to the mayor of Rio de Janeiro, the next city to host the Games.

Athletes from Britain and all over the world are now looking forward to the 2016 Olympics in Rio! It's going to be a big party!

London Olympic Games 2012
Team GB Gold Medal Winners

All team medals are counted as only one, so although 48 gold medals were handed out to British athletes only 29 are counted in the overall standings.

Cycling: Road Cycling

Athlete	Event
Bradley Wiggins	Men's Individual Time Trial

Cycling: Track Cycling

Athlete	Event
(Sir) Chris Hoy	Men's Keirin
Jason Kenny	Men's Sprint
Steven Burke Ed Clancy Peter Kennaugh Geraint Thomas	Men's Team Pursuit
Philip Hindes (Sir) Chris Hoy Jason Kenny	Men's Team Sprint
Victoria Pendleton	Women's Keirin
Laura Trott	Women's Omnium
Dani King Joanna Rowsell Laura Trott	Women's Team Pursuit

Athletics

Athlete	Event
Mo Farah	Men's 10,000m
Mo Farah	Men's 5,000m
Greg Rutherford	Men's Long Jump
Jessica Ennis	Women's Heptathlon

Equestrian

Athlete	Event
Charlotte Dujardin	Individual Dressage
Laura Bechtolsheimer Charlotte Dujardin Carl Hester	Team Dressage
Scott Brash Peter Charles Ben Maher Nick Skelton	Team Jumping

Canoe: Slalom

Athlete	Event
Tim Baillie Etienne Stott	Men's Canoe Double (C2)

Canoe: Sprint

Athlete	Event
Ed McKeever	Men's Kayak Single (K1) 200m

Boxing

🏅 Athlete	Event
Luke Campbell	Men's Bantamweight (56kg)
Anthony Joshua	Men's Super Heavyweight (+91kg)
Nicola Adams	Women's Flyweight (51kg)

Triathalon

🏅 Athlete	Event
Alistair Brownlee	Men's Triathalon

Rowing

🏅 Athlete	Event
Alex Gregory Tom James Pete Reed Andrew Triggs Hodge	Men's Four
Katherine Grainger Anna Watkins	Women's Double sculls
Katherine Copeland Sophie Hosking	Women's Lightweight Double Sculls
Helen Glover Heather Stanning	Women's Pair

Sailing

🏅 Athlete	Event
Ben Ainslie	Men's Finn

Shooting

Athlete	Event
Peter Wilson	Men's Double Trap

Taekwondo

Athlete	Event
Jade Jones	Women's (57kg)

Tennis

Athlete	Event
Andy Murray	Men's Singles

Gold Medals by Sport

Athletics	= 4	
Boxing	= 3	
Canoe	= 2	
Cycling	= 8	
Equestrian	= 3	
Rowing	= 4	
Sailing	= 1	
Shooting	= 1	
Taekwondo	= 1	
Tennis	= 1	
Triathlon	= 1	**= 29**